Roller Hockey

Bill Gutman

Reading consultant:

John Manning, Professor of Reading

University of Minnesota

Capstone Press

MINNEAPOLIS

C A P S T O N E   P R E S S

2440 Fernbrook Lane • Minneapolis, Minnesota 55447

Printed in the United States of America.

Library of Congress Cataloging-in-Publication Data
Gutman, Bill.
    Roller hockey / by Bill Gutman.
    p. cm.
    Includes bibliographical references and index.
    ISBN 1-56065-250-0
    1. Roller-skate hockey--Juvenile literature. I. Title.
GV859.7.G886 1995
796.2'1--dc20

                                        94-31759
                                            CIP
                                              AC

Cover: Chris Lange, a member of the Simi Valley Roller Hockey League, handles the puck with flair. Photo courtesy of Rich Graham.

ISBN: 1-56065-250-0

Table of Contents

Chapter 1

In-Line Excitement

In-line roller hockey may be the hottest new sport of the 1990s. It combines the excitement and speed of ice hockey with the fun of in-line skating. It's a great team game and a great way to improve your skill on in-line skates.

Former ice-hockey stars now compete in a professional roller-hockey league. Bryan Trottier, who helped the New York Islanders win four Stanley Cups, plays roller hockey for the Pittsburgh Phantoms.

In some ways, ice hockey and roller hockey are different. Roller hockey teams have four skaters, instead of five, and a goalie. And there is very little hitting in amateur roller hockey. It's a fun, wide-open game.

Like ice-hockey players, roller-hockey players need speed, stickhandling skills, and skating ability. If you already enjoy in-line skating, roller hockey may be the sport for you.

A Little Background

The first in-line skates were developed by two brothers from Minnesota, Scott and Brennan Olson. They were ice-hockey players who wanted to practice during the summer, when there was no ice.

Even before in-line skates came along, kids were playing a different kind of roller hockey. They used four-wheel roller skates to play on city playgrounds. A rubber ball became the **"puck,"** and broomsticks took the place of hockey sticks.

In-Line Roller Hockey Begins

When in-line skating started booming, roller hockey boomed right along with it. The game was different with in-line skates than with the old roller skates. Players could skate faster. They could start and turn quicker and handle the puck better. In-line skates quickly became the skate of choice for roller-hockey players.

Roller-hockey leagues started in California. New leagues are now forming everywhere. A professional league plays in 18 cities in the United States and Canada. The National In-Line Hockey Association (NIHA) organizes and promotes the sport. It looks like roller hockey will keep growing right into the 21st century.

Chapter 2

Equipment
You Will Need

To play roller hockey, the first thing you need is a pair of in-line skates. Good skates are not cheap, but you should buy the best pair you can afford. It is important to buy skates with a "hinged cuff" (the cuff is the top part of the skate). This gives your feet a little more freedom to move.

Roller-hockey players also like to "rocker" their skates. This means adjusting the two middle wheels so they are slightly higher than the front and rear wheels. **Rockering** allows a player to turn and pivot better. Not all skates can be rockered. Make sure that yours can.

Light Equipment is Best

Speed is important in roller hockey, so the equipment must be very light. Skaters go all out when they play the game. They don't want heavy equipment to slow them down. Always make sure the equipment you buy is as light as possible.

Roller-hockey players under 18 must wear helmets with a full face cage or a clear face shield. Helmets are made of a lightweight plastic and usually have a faceguard. Other required equipment includes a mouth guard or mouthpiece, elbow pads, hockey gloves, knee and shin protectors, and an athletic supporter and protective cup for boys.

Because there is no checking or hitting in roller hockey, shoulder and hip pads are not required. Players older than 18 must wear the same protective equipment except for the face cage or shield.

Pucks and Sticks

Roller hockey is played with either a hard rubber puck or ball. The puck or ball is lighter than a rubber ice-hockey puck but is still dangerous when flying through the air. That's why players wear facemasks and **goalkeepers** wear chest protectors.

Sticks can be no longer than 62 inches (1.58 meters) from the heel (the spot at which the **blade** is attached) to the top of the **shaft**. The blade cannot be more than 12 inches (30 centimeters) wide. The blade also cannot be thicker than 3.25 inches (8.26 centimeters) or thinner than 1.75 inches (4.45 centimeters) at any point. Nor can it have a

curve of more than three-quarters of an inch (1.9 centimeters).

Players should take good care of their equipment. A coach can advise you on this. The better care you take of your skates, sticks, and padding, the longer they will last.

The Rink

Roller-hockey rinks can be made of asphalt, concrete, wood or interlocking tiles. The ideal size is 180 feet (55 meters) long by 80 feet (24 meters) wide. But the NIHA allows rinks from 145 feet to 200 feet (44 meters to 61 meters) long and 65 feet to 100 feet (20 meters to 30 meters) wide. The border of the rink must be at least 8 inches (20.3 centimeters) and not more than 48 inches (121.8 centimeters) high.

A center line 12 inches (30 centimeters) wide divides the rink in half. A team's goal area is called the **defending zone**. The opposing team's goal area is the **attacking zone**.

With only four players and a goalie on each side, roller hockey is a wide-open fast-paced game.

Players battle for the puck and for position during the opening face-off.

Face-Off Positions

Roller-hockey rinks have five **face-off** circles. In the middle of the center line is a circle two feet (60 centimeters) in diameter. This is where face-offs take place at the beginning of each period and after each goal.

There are also two face-off circles in the middle of each zone.

Official roller-hockey goals are six feet (1.8 meters) high and four feet (1.2 meters) wide. Other sizes can be used, but not in tournaments or in championship games. A **goal line** two inches (5.1 centimeters) wide extends from post to post and continues to the sides of the rink. The distance from the goal line to the back of the rink should be between 10 and 15 feet (3.1 and 4.6 meters).

Chapter 3

The Positions

There are three basic positions in roller hockey: **forward**, **defenseman**, and goalkeeper. Once you learn the basics of each position, you can pick the one that suits you.

Forwards

In roller hockey the two forwards are usually the best scorers and the busiest skaters. They have to sprint the length of the rink many times during a game. They look for breakaways and scoring chances, and they must get back on defense when needed. Forwards must also be good passers. They have to handle the stick well and shoot quickly and accurately.

To play forward, you have to be in great shape. That means you have to do a lot of skating, running, and biking. If you get winded easily, you won't be a good forward.

No player can skate hard for an entire game, so every team has two or three sets of forwards. As in ice hockey, players change "on the fly," while the game continues. Two come out of the game, while two others come in.

Defensemen

Roller-hockey defensemen must also be excellent skaters and stickhandlers. They don't have to be as tough as ice-hockey defensemen, because there is no checking or hard contact. But a defenseman must skate with the forwards and be quick enough to steal the puck.

Defensemen must also force the action. Otherwise, they will be skating backward most

Defensemen can't use body checks, but there's plenty of contact in roller hockey.

Goalies need lightning-quick reflexes to keep the puck out of the net.

of the time. It's hard to keep up with a fast forward while skating backwards. And since defensemen can't use body checks, they have to be quick with their sticks and feet.

Once defensemen get the puck, they must rush up the ice or pass quickly to one of the forwards. If a defenseman has a shot, it must be taken quickly. A defenseman often shoots from further out than the forwards. This often requires a good, hard **slap shot**. When the other team gets the puck, a defenseman must get right back on defense.

Goalkeepers

Goalkeepers must stay calm under pressure. To stop the puck from going into the net, they must also have lightning-quick reflexes.

They can stop it with their stick, with their skates, with their legs, or with their gloves. They can also throw their entire body in front of the puck. How they stop it depends on their position and on the kind of shot.

Roller-hockey goalies don't dive as much as ice-hockey goalies. That's because the roller-hockey puck is lighter than an ice-hockey puck. It curves, drops, and rises more quickly. It also can bounce back for a quicker rebound.

Roller-hockey goalies try to stay up on their skates as much as possible, and give the shooter as small a target as possible. They should dive or go to their knees only when they cannot make the **save** any other way.

Though goalies don't usually skate on the open rink, they should still be excellent skaters. They must move quickly back and forth in front of the net. If they leave the goal to pick up a loose puck, they may have to skate backward to the goal. They cannot take their eyes off the puck, even for a second.

Those are the positions on a roller-hockey team. One is not easier to play than another. But you may find that you can play one position best. When you find it, keep practicing that position so you can become the best player you can be.

Chapter 4
Basic Skills

To play roller hockey, you should already know how to in-line skate. Skating is very important. You should work hard to improve some important skating skills.

Roller-hockey players must skate well forwards and backwards, and they must turn quickly in both directions. They also have to be able to stop and start quickly.

Skaters should move as easily on their skates as they move on their feet. If they can't, they need more practice. If you want to be a roller-hockey star, you can never skate well enough. You can always get better.

Stickhandling

No matter how good a skater you are, you won't be a good roller-hockey player if you can't handle the stick. Here are some basic rules of stickhandling.

Players usually hold one hand near the top of the stick and let the other hand move around. As the player carries the puck, the bottom hand moves up. Players slide their hands lower when they get ready to shoot.

The stick is always held with the fingers, not with the palm of the hand. This is important. By holding the stick with the fingers, a player can make a fast shot just by rolling the wrists.

Carrying the Puck

Learning to carry the puck takes a lot of practice. When players "dribble," they must always keep their heads up. It's like a basketball player not looking at the ball when dribbling up court. If a roller-hockey player looks down at the puck, he or she won't see the rest of the action.

There are two basic ways to carry the puck: side-to-side and front-to-back. With the side-to-side method, the skater moves the puck back and forth, catching it with his stick. In the front-to-back method, the player pushes the puck out ahead of him without pulling it back. In both methods, the player always uses the middle of the blade to control the puck.

Once you learn basic stickhandling skills, you have to practice them. Start slowly and get the feel of the puck on your stick. Gradually skate faster, until you can carry the puck at normal speeds. Then start handling the puck on stops and turns. Try to keep it on the blade while you turn and spin. Then begin **carrying** it again.

Stickhandling is an important skill in roller hockey. You can't play well without it.

Passing

Passing is another skill every player must master. Good stickhandling is important, but players move the puck faster by quick and accurate passes.

Roller hockey is much more than shooting and passing. Players have to stay in position and watch for attacks by the opponent.

Usually, both the passer and player receiving the pass are moving. So the passer must put the puck where his or her teammate will be when the puck gets there. Good players don't aim at teammates when they pass. They must "lead" their teammates, just as a football

A player uses the back-and-forth dribble on a breakaway.

quarterback leads a receiver with a pass downfield.

It takes a lot of practice to make good passes. You must judge the distance to your target, and the speed at which you and your teammate are skating. To learn this, go out with a teammate and practice passing as you skate up and down the rink.

There are several different kinds of passes. With each kind, the puck should be pushed across the surface of the rink. If you bang or slap at it, the puck could rise off the surface and miss the target.

In the **forehand** pass, the puck comes off the inside of the blade. In the **backhand** pass, the puck comes off the outside. For a right-handed skater, the right side of the blade is the backhand side. Forehand and backhand passes can be long or short. So practice them both ways.

Passers should keep their sticks close to the surface and use them to slide the puck. It's important to keep the blade low for the entire pass. If you lift the stick, you may lift the puck off the surface as well.

The **back pass** is a backhand pass that you make to a teammate behind you. It is often used near an opponent's goal, when the other skater has a better shot. Use a simple backward stroke to slide the puck back. But

To defend against the fast shots, roller hockey goalies have to stay up as much as possible.

make sure you know where your teammate and the defenders are before making a back pass.

The **drop pass** may be the simplest. While using front-to-back control, the skater leaves the puck sitting still and continues to skate forward. But there must be a teammate ready to pick up the puck and move it toward the goal.

Receiving Passes

Always hold the stick loosely when you receive a pass. That way, the blade will "give" slightly, making it easier to catch the puck. If you hold the stick tightly, the puck may hit the blade and bounce away.

It may also help to cup the stick. That means laying the blade at an angle over the moving puck. Just make sure you don't lift the stick off the surface and let the puck slide underneath.

Shooting

There are two basic roller-hockey shots: the **wrist shot** and the **slap shot**. The slap shot is a harder shot, but it is not as easy to control. Often, a good wrist shot is the better choice.

With both shots, the shooter puts weight on the front foot. That's the left foot for a right-handed shooter and the right foot for a lefty. The upper hand on the stick directs the shot, while the lower hand gives the shot its power.

The Wrist Shot

The wrist shot is taken with the puck close to the heel, or rear, of the blade. Right-handed shooters snap their left wrist back while the right hand snaps the stick forward. The lefty does it the opposite way. As the wrists are snapped, the shooter shifts weight from the rear to the front foot. He or she follows through by pointing the stick at the target.

A good wrist shooter can lift the puck by cupping the blade over it before taking the shot. This takes a lot of practice. But it also takes practice to get the shot to go where you want it.

The Slap Shot

The slap shot uses a full swing of the stick. With the feet facing the goal and the puck alongside, the shooter raises the stick at least waist high. As the player swings, the weight shifts from the rear to the front foot. The stick should hit the surface just behind the puck. A good follow-through will send the puck screaming toward the goal.

Defensemen prepare as an attacking forward lets fly with a wicked slap shot.

A good slap-shooter also can get the puck to rise. It is important for all players to develop the wrist shot first, then the slap shot. Every team needs good shooters who can take both kinds of shots.

Chapter 5

The Game

Under NIHA rules, there are two ways to time roller-hockey games. There can be two, 22-minute running-time halves with a five-minute halftime rest. "Running time" means the clock doesn't stop during the halves.

Or there can be two, 12- to 15-minute stop-time halves with a five-minute rest. "Stop time" means that the clock stops every time play stops. Each team also can take a one-minute timeout during regulation time.

Basic Strategy

The strategy of roller hockey is very simple. Attacking teams usually come up the rink in either a box or a diamond formation. In the box, both forwards are up front and on the wings (close to the sides of the rink). The defensemen are further back and closer to the middle. All four players move up the rink together, passing the puck and looking for a breakaway.

In the diamond, two players skate on the wings, with a third in the middle and in front. The fourth player is in the middle and behind. Some teams switch quickly from the box to the diamond. Players must make long and accurate passes in both formations.

When the puck gets close to the goal, players begin to cut toward the net. They are looking for a quick pass in close. After the goalie makes a save, they also are in position to put in a rebound.

Fast-Break Game

Some teams also play fast-break hockey. When a player gets the puck deep in his or her own territory, the three others begin to skate rapidly up the rink. The player with the puck makes a long pass to a teammate who is ahead of the defense. After getting the pass, the teammate goes in for a quick shot on goal.

Teamwork is important in all formations. The players must work together as a unit. No player is more important than the team.

Professional Roller Hockey

With age group and amateur leagues springing up all around the country, a professional league had to happen. Roller Hockey International began play in 1993 and in 1994 expanded from 10 to 24 teams. The league is now on television, and several former ice-hockey stars play for the various clubs.

The league uses standard ice-hockey rinks that have various surfaces, from cement to plastic-tiled floors. The season runs from early

June to late September. The commissioner of the league is former Montreal Canadiens star Ralph Backstrom.

Hitting Allowed

Like the amateur version, pro roller hockey uses four skaters and a goalkeeper. There is no high-sticking or fighting, but the league does allow body checking. This will make the games more exciting for TV audiences and fans who are used to ice hockey. There are four 12-minute quarters, and each team has 14 players on its roster.

The teams play in major arenas like the Great Western Forum in Los Angeles, the Spectrum in Philadelphia, and the legendary Montreal Forum. Specially designed pucks are used in all the professional games.

The next page has a list of all the teams playing in 1996. See if there is one close to you.

Roller Hockey International

PACIFIC DIVISION
Anaheim Bullfrogs
San Diego Barracudas
Los Angeles Blades
Oklahoma Coyotes
Denver Daredevils

NORTHWESTERN DIVISION
Vancouver VooDoo
San Jose Rhinos
Sacramento River Rats
Oakland Skates

CENTRAL DIVISION
Montreal Roadrunners
St. Louis Vipers
Minnesota Arctic Blast
Ottawa Rolar Bears

ATLANTIC DIVISION
Long Island Jawz
New Jersey Rockin Rollers
Philadelphia Bulldogs
Empire State Cobras
Orlando Jackals

There are also plans to start another professional league in Japan. The sport is spreading around the world, and it looks as if roller hockey is here to stay. You can be part of it!

Glossary

attacking zone–the area of the rink where the offensive or attacking team tries to score

backhand–a shot or pass made with the outside edge of the stick's blade

back pass–a backward pass made by a skater to a teammate skating behind him or her

blade–the part of the hockey stick that touches the surface of the rink and that controls the puck

carrying–to move the puck forward with the hockey stick. Also called dribbling

defending zone–the area where the defensive or defending team tries to stop its opponents from scoring

defenseman–a player whose job is to stop the opposing forwards from scoring

drop pass–the pass in which a player leaves the puck for a teammate skating right behind him or her

face-off–the method of putting the puck in play. The referee drops the puck between two opposing players who try to gain control.

forehand–a shot or pass made with the inside edge of the stick's blade

forward–one of two players on the rink whose primary job is to move the puck toward the opposition goal and score

goalkeeper–the player who guards the goal and stops opposing shots from going into the net

goal line–a two-inch-wide line that runs between the goalposts and extends to each side of the rink

puck–the flat round disk that both teams try to control and shoot into the net

rockering–raising slightly the middle two wheels of an in-line skate. This makes it easier to turn and pivot on the skates

save–to stop a shot from going in the net

shaft–the thin portion of the hockey stick to which the blade is attached. The player holds the stick by the shaft

slap shot–a hard shot made by raising the stick off the surface and then bringing it down to strike the puck

wrist shot–a more controlled shot in which the stick remains on the surface and pushes the puck toward the goal

To Learn More

Gutman, Bill. *Blazing Bladers*. New York, NY: Tor Books, 1992.

Joyner, Steven Christopher. *The Complete Guide and Resource to In-Line Skating*. Cincinnati, OH: Betterway Books, 1993.

Martin, John. *In-Line Skating*. Minneapolis, MN: Capstone Press, 1994.

Sullivan, George. *In-Line Skating, A Complete Guide for Beginners*. New York, NY: Cobblehill Books, 1993.

Roller Hockey Magazine
12327 Santa Monica Blvd., Suite 202
Los Angeles, CA 90025

Hockey Talk
40575 California Oaks Road
#D2255
Murrieta, CA 92562

Some Useful Addresses

The National In-Line Hockey Association is an independent organization focused on the development, organization, and promotion of amateur in-line hockey. For more information call NIHA: (305) 358-8988 or write:

**National In-Line Hockey Association
  U.S. Headquarters**
999 Brickell Avenue
Ninth Floor
Miami, FL 33131

**National In-Line Hockey Association
  Canadian Headquarters**
11810 Kingsway
Edmonton, AB T5G 0X5
Canada
(403) 455-NIHA

Index